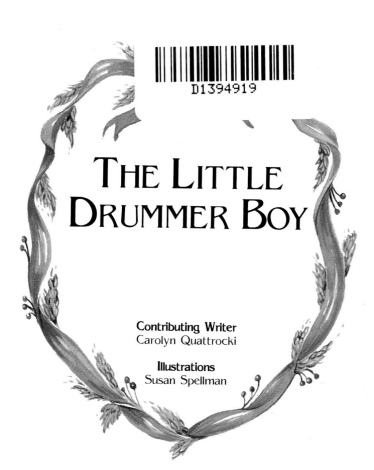

THE LITTLE DRUMMER BOY

Contributing Writer
Carolyn Quattrocki

Illustrations
Susan Spellman

Publications International, Ltd.

A long time ago, near the town of Bethlehem, lived a little boy. His family was very poor.

The boy had one thing that made his life happy. He had a drum. Years before, when his grandfather was young, a group of traveling musicians had come to the little village. They gave his grandfather the drum.

When the little boy was old enough, he learned to play *pa-rum pum pum pum*. Now the drum belonged to him.

The little boy loved his drum more than anything in the world. He played it every day all around his village. The other children would follow behind him, marching and singing as he played.

The people in the village began to call him the Little Drummer Boy. They smiled when they heard him playing and singing:

Pa-rum pum pum pum.

At the same time, in a town called Nazareth, there lived a young woman named Mary. One day, an angel told Mary that she would have a son, Jesus.

Now, Caesar Augustus, the ruler of the land, ordered all the people to go to the town where they were born. There, the tax collectors would count them.

So Mary and her husband, Joseph, set out for Bethlehem. Mary was expecting her baby soon.

When Mary and Joseph finally arrived in Bethlehem, it was crowded with all the people who had come to be counted. Joseph looked and looked for a place to spend the night, but no one had room for them.

Finally, one innkeeper said, "I have no room inside, but there is a stable behind the inn where you could stay overnight."

Mary and Joseph were so tired they were happy to have any place to spend the night.

During the night, the baby was born. Mary named the boy Jesus. She made a bed for him by putting him in a manger.

That same night, some shepherds were out in the fields. Suddenly, an angel appeared and told them about Jesus. The angel told the shepherds to go to Bethlehem.

Then many angels appeared and sang, "Peace on earth and good will to all." When the angels left, the shepherds hurried to see the baby Jesus.

Everyone was talking about baby Jesus and wanted to bring him gifts. The Little Drummer Boy wanted to see Jesus, too, but what present could he give?

That night, he saw a most wonderful sight. In front of him were three kings carrying beautiful gifts.

The Little Drummer Boy listened as he followed them. "There is the star we follow," said one. "See, it points us toward the stable up ahead."

The three kings followed the star to the stable where the baby Jesus lay in a manger.

"My name is Melchior," said the first. "I have brought a gift of gold for the baby." The second said, "I am Gaspar. I have brought frankincense, a rare perfume." "And my name is Balthazar," said the third. "I, too, have brought a valuable perfume, called myrrh."

The three kings laid their gifts before the manger.

The Little Drummer Boy was sad that he had no gift. But he started playing and singing:

Come they told me,
*   pa-rum pum pum pum,*

Our newborn King to see,
*   pa-rum pum pum pum.*

Our finest gifts we bring,
*   pa-rum pum pum pum,*

To lay before the King,
*   pa-rum pum pum pum,*

So to honor Him,
*   pa-rum pum pum pum,*

When we come.

Baby Jesus,
  pa-rum pum pum pum,
I am a poor boy, too,
  pa-rum pum pum pum.
I have no gift to bring,
  pa-rum pum pum pum,
That's fit to give a king,
  pa-rum pum pum pum.
Shall I play for you,
  pa-rum pum pum pum,
On my drum?

Baby Jesus smiled at the boy.
Everyone in the stable knew
that the boy was giving the
best gift of all—the gift of love.